HORRID
little
STORIES

SIXTY DARK AND TINY TALES OF MISERY AND WOE

by DAVID MALKI !

The author of
WONDERMARK.COM

A BEARSTACHE POCKETBOOK
Bearstache Books, Venice, Calif.

THE WONDERMARK COLLECTION

includes:

THE ANNOTATED WONDERMARK
ISBN 978-0-9821671-0-6

BEARDS OF OUR FOREFATHERS
ISBN 978-1-939768-00-1

CLEVER TRICKS TO STAVE OFF DEATH
ISBN 978-1-939768-01-8

DAPPER CAPS & PEDAL-COPTERS
ISBN 978-1-5958244-9-3

EMPEROR OF THE FOOD CHAIN
ISBN 978-1-936561-93-3

DISPATCHES FROM WONDERMARK MANOR
ISBN 978-0-9821671-5-1

CLASSY LADY LIKE YOU WILL LOVE THE SMELL OF MY BUTT
ISBN 978-0-9821671-9-9

Available Wherever Books Are Sold

If your local bookmonger is out, visit TOPATOCO.COM/WONDERMARK for "internet" commerce featuring all the charm of monetary exchange with none of the perils of human interaction. You will also find there a full list of Wondermark brand dry-goods and gift items, which are good.

HORRID LITTLE STORIES

Copyright © 2014 by David Malki ! All rights reserved.

ISBN 978-1-939768-04-9
Printed in the United States of America
Second printing : November 2014

The pages to come
    feature nothing of taste

For those whose opinions discern;

It's vileness, crudity,
    gross and debased

As in a few moments you'll learn.

I wrote these small ditties
    in calendar form

And printed them every December;

Hence there are references
    (I should inform

you) to matters you may
    not remember.

For each little verse is a
    statement of fact,

For each page, my
    research meticulous;

The details recounted
    are true and exact

Your doubts—I'll just say—
    are ridiculous.

the WONDERMARK 2008 calendar.

Featuring Twelve Tales of Love, Loss and Mourning Offering Grim Hope for the Year to Come.

The year started off on the
   darkest of notes

When Grace found a drink
   in the cellar.

A potion she thought was a
   balm for her throat—

One sip was sufficient
   to fell her.

The doctor declared it
   a mild offense

But cautioned against
   our elation:

"Go lay down some plastic
   before I dispense

The cure for her fierce
   constipation."

For twenty long years Franklin
    wished his wife dead

But fear of the law
    kept him civil.

Till one afternoon Franklin
    craftily said:

"We've no need for
    Valentine drivel!"

She stopped slicing beets
    as he summoned a snort:

"I'm sure you'll agree
    it's absurd?"

She shrieked—and he smiled
    through her stabbing retort

A self-defense plea
    now assured.

"These holes in your boots
    will be costly to patch,"

The cobbler declared
    with a sneer.

"It's bad for the soles,
    using them to dispatch

Those pests in your garden
    each year."

"I'll stomp what I wish,"
    Marvin bellowed with zeal,

"Alternative methods are slow.

Just patch up the leaks,
    for I don't wish to feel

Warm leprechaun brains
    in my toes!"

The statements each month
   left Mathilda dejected—

All bankruptcy, failure and ruin.

But Sam cheered her up
   with a quite unexpected

Proposal that seemed
   worth pursuing.

He claimed they'd earn millions
   in one easy stunt

With rather peculiar criteria:

"To access the money,
   we'll need some up front—

Just wire the funds to Nigeria."

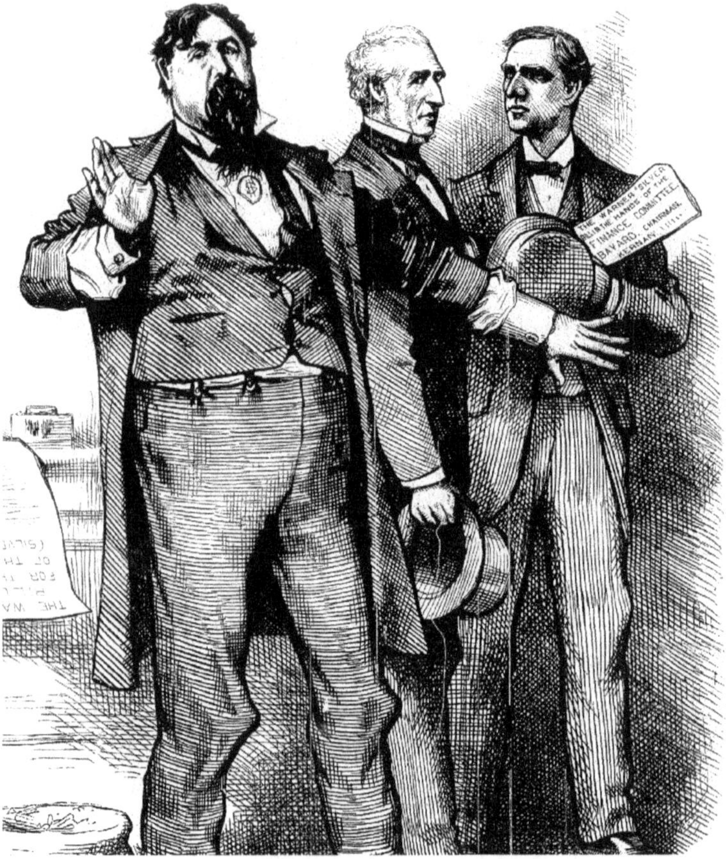
THE WARNER "SILVER
BILL IN THE HANDS OF THE
"FINANCE" COMMITTEE.
BAYARD, CHAIRMAN
KERNAN

The Senator flaunted
  his walrus moustache;
He claimed it equipped
  him with vigor.
His rivals despised his
  near-peerless panache
Impregnable each way
  they figured.
They crept out at midnight
  to shave off his pride
With razors and ether
  for numbing;
He slew them with buckshot
  'fore one got inside
His whiskers had known
  they were coming.

The Army stormed into
   the nobleman's manse
The day of the peasantry coup.
Poor Jim was so nervous
     he soiled his pants
His first day of soldiering, too.
He slashed through the couches
     with his bayonet
And otherwise went on
     with looting,
The whole time his trousers
     uncomfortably wet—
They'd not mentioned this
     in recruiting.

How fireworks burn
   in that patriot air!

The brilliant display
   starts at nine.

But come to the park
   with an hour to spare

For a show you'd be mad
   to decline.

Old Scruffy McCabe's
   got a Redcoat brigade

Made of terriers decked out
   in britches.

The dogs all parade
   even though they're unpaid

'Cause back home he's got guns
   to their bitches.

When Franzio brandished
    his cane at the door

The waiters all let out a groan.

His sneer was familiar
    (from visits before)

His dissatisfaction well-known.

"Don't spit in my chowder,
    you know I'm no dupe,"

He hollered, expecting a joke;

With torrents of insults
    he sent back his soup—

Then drank down the pee
    in his Coke.

Marcellus rebelled at
 a typical age
From parents' well-wishes
 he fled;
Rejecting the concept of
 working for wage
He took up the fiddle instead.
With decades of labor,
 he's mastered the skill
And lives for the favor it draws
But now and again he regrets
 his choice still—
You can't pay the rent
 with applause.

McHenry's contention was
    that the convention

Of Halloween "tricking"
    was lost.

To aid its retention, he
    cashed in his pension

For a kilt and some
    argyle socks.

Should treats be denied
    he took time to decide

What retributive method
    was best:

Until they complied,
    he'd expose his backside—

But he hadn't expected requests.

The yams in my toothpaste
    I chalked up to fluke;

I shrugged when the
    shower shot broth.

But peeing out gravy spelled
    "bonafide spook"

So I called in a man of the cloth.

He knew right away:
    "Angry spirits been killed!"

What courage I'd had,
    I soon lost—

"You're haunted by turkeys!"
    he shrieked, and I filled

My undies with
    cranberry sauce.

Between every catalog,
   store and boutique
Jill had just a single request.
Its flattering figure would
   shape her physique
No matter what ribs
   it compressed.
So come Christmas morning
   she squealed with delight
Right into the corset
   she squeezed;
She wouldn't admit that
   it fit rather tight
But exploded the first time
   she sneezed.

This calendar's written
   a year in advance
And who knows what
   the future will bring us?
My guess is by now we'll have
   nuked half of France
And the South will have
   banned cunnilingus.
The oceans will drown all the
   valuable beaches
Where rich people love to
   go jogging;
Bin Laden will open a school
   where he teaches
The art of interpretive clogging.

The moon will reveal
> it's in fact made of cheese

Making hunger no longer
> an issue;

The leading importer will be
> the Chinese

So the dollar will double
> for tissue.

As all the world sinks
> into wanton perversion

A single solution is clear:

If you've been amused by
> this monthly diversion

Please buy a new version
> next year!

WONDERMARK 2009

*An Ephemeris in Jest and Earnest,
Containing Merry Tales,
Humorous Poetry, Whims,
Oddities, &c.*

"This year is the one!"
　　Chester let out a roar,

"I'm pumped for my
　　new resolution!"

Young Leo just nodded.
　　He'd seen this before.

Intentions, but no execution.

Since Chester was weak, well,
　　his friend would be stronger

A buttress when
　　discipline crumbles—

For Chester's next workout
　　would last even longer

Once Leo put glue
　　on the dumbbells.

The girl from his neighborhood
   seemed pretty swell

At dinner, a positive jester;

And since the whole evening
   was going so well

He showed her his toy
   to impress her.

She sat at the eyepiece
   to find it still hot

And leapt right back up,
   arms akimbo;

So busy he'd been that
   he'd clearly forgot

The scope was still aimed
   at her window.

"We'll take the whole lot!"
    came the man's affirmation,

Inspecting his purchase
    with surety.

The artist's heart leapt!
    For this fine validation

Would rescue his name
    from obscurity.

"Their value will rise,"
    he enlightened the client,

"Please get them appraised,
    so your heir knows."

"I don't think we'll bother,"
    the man said, defiant,

"They're going straight out
    to be scarecrows."

Armand was allergic
 to something or other

That phlegmed up his
 trunk with congestion;

The elephant doctors
 disputed each other

And offered conflicting
 suggestions.

First he tried opium;
 that caused psychosis

And Prozac just made him
 hate living;

He finally settled on booze
 in such dosage

To knock him out
 clear 'til Thanksgiving.

On Mother's Day morning
    José had a plan

A gift from a clever young mind:

For twenty-four hours,
    a model young man!

Obedient, pleasant and kind.

That evening his mother
    began to inspect

The boy's scalp or his spine
    for the scars

To prove what today
    she had come to suspect—

That this well-behaved
    child was from Mars.

Jerome was a pensive
 biology teacher

Who put little stock
 in mythology.

Till far out to sea he
 discovered a creature

Of interest to cryptozoology.

The serpent was strong,
 to our hero's chagrin;

The dinghy near flipped
 from their struggle!

Jerome was afraid,
 but he needn't have been—

It was lonely, and
 just wanted snuggles.

Lieutenant Muldoon
 was to lead an inspection—

His first since his
 brand-new promotion.

He asked Sergeant Boone
 for a bit of direction

As he'd not the foggiest notion.

"The thing 'bout inspections
 is no one's immune,"

Said Sarge, 'fore the man
 could think twice;

The rest of the day
 the entire platoon

Methodically checked him
 for lice.

A tramp and his dog!
   No more nobler sight!

Detritus of urbanization—

Such transient souls
   cannot fail to ignite

A wanderlust borne
   of frustration.

"I'm trapped!" thinks the
   middle-class would-be
   bohème

Observing the comrades
   with yearning;

But hitting the road
   in a manner like them

Doesn't pay what he'd
   rather be earning.

"Geometry! Surely I'll use
 that a lot,"
Remarked Cain to the stodgy
 old dean.
He gazed down his nose
 at the relics who thought
They knew better than he,
 at sixteen.
"Ignore at your peril,"
 the dean simply shrugged;
"If that's how you feel,
 be obtuse!"
That *was* how Cain felt—
 up until he was mugged
By a renegade hypotenuse.

Claire was too fragile
 for Halloween night—

All the monsters caused
 fits of anxiety.

Mother tried setting her
 poor angel right

With a misguided bid
 for sobriety.

"There's no need to tremble
 at make-believe threats

When so many valid abound!

'Tween cancer, and war, and
 Peak Oil, and our debts…"

Now Claire is a wreck
 all year round.

The jerk spat an insult
    regarding her weight

But should have been
    looking around—

The bridge railing shattered.
    The coach hit the bay.

Samantha just watched
    the man drown.

A wry Schadenfreude
    I wouldn't begrudge her—

How mocking and mean
    had his laughter been!

A crowd soon collected, but
    they wouldn't judge her;

It's not like they thought
    she'd dive after him.

He'd long stopped believing
 in jolly red elves

And in reindeer with
 magical skills—

But that Christmas Eve he would
 swear he'd heard *bells!*

And that *laugh!* Oh, it gave
 him the chills!

He tried to stay silent
 as downward he crept

His adrenaline high,
 his hope soaring—

He saw that red suit
 and his heart! How it leapt!

But alas. Just a burglary. *Boring.*

The end of the year! And
the end of these pages—

Convenient they happen
    in tandem.

While Time does appear
    to persist through the ages,

The calendar's somewhat
    more random.

I'm sure I'll be here at the
    same time next year

Composing these verses again;

If you'll say the same,
    and then honor that claim,

Let's make it a date for oh-ten.

WONDERMARK 2010

A Forlorn Collection of Whimsical Tales, Intended (but not Approved) for the Instruction of YOUTH, ADULTS & THE CRIMINALLY INSANE

The novelist put in to do
 a ride-along with cops;

He figured that the grim and
 gritty beat would be the tops

To give his stories honest flavor
 and his tales the ring of truth;

(Besides, the Sarge owed him a
 favor.) He was off to be a sleuth!

The first day was surprising—
 his presumptions proved untrue;

He ended up revising everything
 he thought he knew.

And yet it wasn't till the end, when
 glad goodbyes were being said

That he learned the Sarge had sent
 him to the clown college instead.

"O *magnifique* beard! Far the
  best I have seen!
Such glory I've never espied!
To bask in its majesty:
  my fondest dream!
Within it I'd gladly reside."

The bearded one halted
  as if in distress
"It's not quite as it
  might appear;
Your praise is a kindness,
  but I must confess
That in truth, it's the
  beard of my beard."

The Gentlemen of Sport
　　rejected Peter's application

To join a league or swab a court
　or work administration;

Despite his clear enthusiasm
　for the club objectives

And memorizing through-and-
　through the list of club directives

Now it's not that Peter wasn't
　quite the sporting type, in fact;

And it wasn't that his eyesight
　was so poor (just inexact);

'Twas that all their sweaty strutting
　was to get girls in the mood,

And poor Peter's fanbase, soup to
　nuts, was crabby Aunt Gertrude.

Each tax-day Maurice
   grew depressingly solemn

Those dollar amounts
   seemed so *mocking!*

A single stray decimal,
   a mis-sorted column,

And auditors soon
   would come knocking.

But all of his work
   seemed a ceaseless abyss

So on one day he *gave up*
   his taxing:

"What *more* could they do?
   That'd be worse than *this?*"

But soon he regretted the axing.

Bernard was smashed by half past
  two each day (if not by noon)

The family gnashed their teeth and
  knew this had to end, and soon.

An intervention went ahead
  as led by Aunt Maureen:

Bernard was led into a shed
  where waited this machine.

"And this will wean me off the
  booze?" he said, scanning its
  shape;

Dear Auntie simply took his shoes
  to preempt an escape.

"Its aim is most precise," she said,
  "its painlessness top-drawer;

You'll feel a tiny slice about the
  neck—but not much more."

"We're ready to fight!"
　　came the warrior's boast,
Our blood and our blades
　　call for battle—
And should any enemy
　　try to riposte
We'll slaughter their army
　　like cattle."

"Preposterous rot!" an
　　onlooker complained
"There's no shred of sense
　　in what you say!"

"It's none of your business,"
　　the soldier explained,
"What Pam and I do
　　when we role-play."

Michelle's new baby seemed a rather strange and
  freakish puzzle;

It wore a coat of creamy fur
  and, irrefutably, a muzzle.

Perhaps a mix-up at the nursery,
  or worse, a foolish joke;

The nurse had given him a cursory
  inspection (just a poke)

So it was possible that someone
  slipped this beast into her stroller

And now was having twisted fun
  while Emma Lou tried to console her:

"Is the father packing genes that might
  be odd—Oh, what do I know?"

Only *then* Michelle remembered that
  immodest week in Cairo.

"My friend, I've seen combat
    from France to Ceylon

A new deadly threat
    every minute;

Assassins—mad bombers—
    oh, I could go on

Just hand me a war
    and I'll win it.

Since being a hero is
    clearly my lot,

I'm sure you are
    duly impressed—"

The Colonel stopped cold. "I say,
    what's that you've got?"

"Oh! A shovel for all your B.S."

The first-ever journey
    through flux-warping space
Involved physics in
    forty dimensions;
A nationwide search found
    that only young Grayson
Had adequate
    math comprehension.
He insisted on doing it all
    in his head
Asserting his skills analytical;
He probably should have
    used paper instead
His error was small
    but quite critical.

I peer into your bedrooms
  and observe you in your beds

I'm enchanted by your costumes
  and the fabric on your heads

You humans are so darling!
  Oh, I *love* to watch you sleeping!

But I am met with snarling, shouts
  of rage, and wretched weeping;

I really don't quite follow
  what could ever be the hurdle

As I travel like Apollo coolly
  gazing at your girdles

I chose a form that's cheerful;
  the result of much research—

So why are folks so fearful when
  I emerge over their church?

"Three hats for one!" Arturo smirked,
"Down at the pier they've gone berserk
Now listen, man, the sale is on
Another hour and they'll be gone
This three-hat deal won't last all day
So get a move on! Don't delay!"
But Lance just stood there. Didn't move.
"I don't know how I could improve
On my existing hat. I *love* it!
So you can take your sale and shove it."
Arturo fumed. "You can't say that!
I found a *deal* for *several hats!*
I'm being *frugal!* More than y'all!
And everyone who sees you crawl
These city streets with one hat on
Will fight to stifle several yawns!
Now Lance, you dolt, here's one more chance
To buy *three hats* for the change in your pants!"
Arturo sometimes played the pest
Explaining how his way was best
But Lance just smiled at his abuse.
His hat was fine. Did *theirs* make juice?

"Pretend that I'm blind,"
    said Melissa to Ken,

"I want to conduct an inspection."

She felt up his face,
    then she did it again—

Then she *shivered*
    at some imperfection.

"What is it?" said Ken,
    thinking all was a gas,

Not noticing how she'd gone pale;

His pockmarks and scars—
    oh, their terrible mass!—

Spelled out sick innuendoes
    in Braille.

Two thousand ten!
  Just watch it go!

It fled so very fast

(I'm guessing here,
  'cause as you know

I'm writing
  from the past.)

Oh no! A thought!
  Perhaps I'm *dead*

A year from when
  I'm writing

It's possible you
  have just read

My *final words.*
  Exciting!

Attacked by an
    old dog, perhaps,

Or by a tiger bitten;

With dying breath:
    "At least," I gasp,

"The calendar got written."

If any joy you
    did derive

From said, now
    thus completed;

Should I, in fact
    (somehow) survive

Till next year—
    I'll repeat it.

A MISERABLE COMPENDIUM *of* Vicious Rhymes, Unpleasant Accounts, and General Malfeasance

Utterly Deleterious to the Common Good — Fit Only for Scorn.

Sam took on the Amazon
 like Gulliver in Lilliput;

Romping, causing damage, for no
 reason but to mess things up.

He shot a monkey, punched a bird,
 and stole a baby's candy;

He broke a native's MacBook
 and replaced it with a Tandy.

—And then one day he disappeared!
 Just not there anymore.

The only sign he left behind:
 a messy mound of gore

That curiously had followed
 fervent prayers to the Madonna

That all Sam's blood cells, every one,
 be turned into piranha.

Lenore bought a book
   on becoming productive

And read the whole thing
   in a night.

Adored it, and took away
   tons of instructive

Suggestions to set herself right.

She set her alarm for
   Ambitous O'Clock

Determined to cast off
   her fetters;

Ten snooze-buttons later
   she called it all off.

Perhaps the next book
   would be better.

Coffee addiction
    made trouble for Sue;

The jitters just made her
    work slower.

And constant, repeated,
    trips up to the loo

Would sink her efficiency lower.

When she then conceived
    of a novel technique

Even her inner voice
    laughed at her;

But she started saving
    ten hours a week

Simply by wearing a catheter.

Anna asked Mercutio the
Goldfish-Man to marry her.

She said "From your imprisonment
beneath the sea, you're freed!"

The contrast in their respiration
frankly did not worry her;

She flooded her apartment
so her fiancé could breathe.

The wedding was adorable;
a puffer-fish officiated!

He gave in to her wishes,
as a doting husband does;

But never quite could meet her
on the level that she operated

Since every thirty seconds
he forgot just who she was.

A child left alone
    in a mall after hours

With all of the stores
    shut up tight

Has nothing to do
    but pretend he has powers

Like speed, X-ray vision,
    and flight.

He runs to and fro on
    the wide, vacant aisles,

Unhindered by shoppers
    or teens;

—Trips, takes a spill, and
    down there on the tiles

Learns what *alone* truly means.

As dusk begins to paint
  the far horizon shades of red

The denizens of daylight
  step aside for night instead.

Of wendigoes and werewolves,
  ghosts and witches, you well know;

But a novel kind of monster
  was just born not long ago.

It's got tentacles aplenty,
  horns and fangs across its face;

One eye that sees the devil,
  and another just in case.

It haunts children in their
  nightmares, drawing blood
  with each attack;

Then it showers, has some tea, and
  goes to work at Goldman Sachs.

Alphonse had a morbid
    adventurous streak:

He loved to investigate killings.

He'd check out a crypt
    any day of the week;

A trip to the morgue he
    found thrilling.

His friends, growing tired
    of his constant fixation,

Set desperate plans into motion:

They treated Alphonse to a
    "shipwreck vacation"

(Then set him adrift on the ocean.)

Where he died

Pierre the gourmand
had a rarified taste;

Each bite on his plate,
a new flavor.

His fine staff of chefs
incessantly faced

The challenge of
meeting his favor.

Till they found *The Meat*.
  So delicious! So soft!

Each cut sent Pierre into spasm:

"What an outstanding feat!
  O my cap, it is doffed!

Between this and all others—
  a chasm!"

With the next bite he toppled.
  Fell drained of his life.

The chefs traded glances
  and smiled;

They'd opened a *time-portal*
  under his knife—

He'd eaten himself as a child.

The prince's new kitten,
   the Lady JoAnn

Was given a seat in the royalty.

Thoroughly smitten,
   the silly *dauphin*

Presumed a reciprocal loyalty.

But she was aloof, as a
   cat tends to be;

By and by, she stopped
   coming around.

So he wrote a decree:
   "I *demand* you love me!"

(Her reply was to barf
   on his crown.)

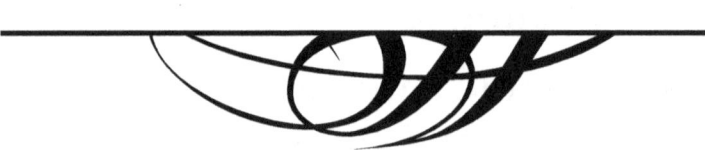

The tons of food we throw away
 give life to certain beasts!

In sewers, slums and alley-ways,
 upon our meals they feast.

A peel's a meal, a fry's a prize,
 a pretzel stick's a pleasure;

They fight to lick an empty milk-jug
 caked with liquid treasure.

A mold-encrusted sourdough
 provides their penicillin;

It doesn't taste like much, although
 at least it's rather filling.

How miserable to live this way!
 And be depressed they oughta—

But they don't care, because of all
 the Prozac in the water.

Fifty small rodents
 live in my pants!

They scurry about;
 keep me warm.

They pick off small insects,
 aphids and ants;

And mend where my
 trousers are torn.

I like them a lot!
 I think they are rad.

They're my brothers—
 or at least my cousins.

But I don't give them names,
 so I don't feel too sad

When I sit down and
 crush a few dozen.

The latest, the best, every
    gadget there is:

Pete was entirely hooked.

Next-gen; GPS; if it's new,
    then it's his—

Version 1 bugs overlooked.

His toaster used Bluetooth
    to brown distant bread;

Worked great—but for
    one little catch

A glitch in the firmware
    browned Pete in his bed

(The developers issued a patch).

What do you do when
a calendar is done?

Try to flip it over and
 give it another run?

The dates will be a little off,
 the holidays askew;

But with some mental math you
 make adjustments—good as new!

Still, you take a gamble,
 and in stressful situations

A misreading of the calendar
 can have dire complications.

Better not to risk it—after all
 it isn't hard

To simply buy a new one for
 two thousand twelve! —*Regards.*

WONDERMARK 2012

A Disagreeable Compilation of
GROTESQUE ANECDOTES

OF NO USE TO THE UPRIGHT CITIZEN
BUT A POSITIVE BOON TO THE WRETCHED.

Is this the year Imaginary Day
shows up at last?

February 30th! I've waited
for the past

Four hundred years since old Pope
Gregory forgot you off his list—

Your absence has been noticed and
your presence has been missed!

I like that you're an underdog,
'cause I feel like one too.

I like that you keep trying, though
the odds are stacked against you.

I'm always disappointed when I
wake on first of March;

You're never on the calendars, but
always in my heart.

Dr. McSnooze was the rational type
Not given to wild speculation;
He didn't believe any media hype—
"I'll trust peer-reviewed publication."
His favorite field was studying sleep
The subject of rest, his dominion:
See, when his alarm said "Get up! On your feet!"
He'd wait for a second opinion.

Sixty sailors set out to subdue
 the seven seas

Forty made it to a stormy island;

Thirty-five sought shelter, racked
 with hunger and disease

By morning, seventeen
 of them lay silent.

Eight succumbed to cholera,
 then seven caught the flu;

And two inflated with
 some kind of bloat

The lone survivor made himself
 a throne out of bamboo—

"I guess we needn't put it to
 a vote!"

"Another rejection! Just kill me!" Bill cried,

Prostrating himself on the chair.

"Now, now," Dee consoled, as she came to his side,

"Don't surrender to writer's despair!"

"But I've met every agent, I've followed each lead,

I've polished my prose and my diction—

I'm beginning to fear that no one wants to read

My Snorks/Guy Fieri fan-fiction!"

She kissed off his tears as he choked off a wail.

She knew this was why God made wives:

"Hush," whispered she. "You just tell me a tale

Of diners, and drive-ins, and dives."

Haydn the Magician fished
 about inside his jacket

Pulling out a dozen knotted flags,

Then there came a rabbit—
 then an eagle to attack it—

Then a pillow, and a full-sized
 sleeping bag.

Each set Daisy clapping,
 gasping brightly with acclaim:

"Smashing! Do another,
 won't you please!"

Haydn took the accolades,
 though that was not his aim;

He just wanted to find
 his freaking keys!

T he portrait was striking.
   The ladies all swooned!

It's like he was actually there!

The details were true, from
   his festering wound

To the four pounds of grease
   in his hair.

They'd captured his blundering
    sense of command,

They'd captured his
    melonesque jaw;

They'd captured his skin color—
    orange and tanned

And gave him his
    cheekful of chaw.

One license they took:
    they gave him a shirt.

(To avoid the appearance
    of crudeness.)

But that was His Highness—
    O ever the flirt,

He insisted you call him
    "His Dudeness."

Gene was a tyrant, the real hell-for-leather type management often attracts.

He'd famously stapled two interns together for "critically wrinkling" a fax.

The wrong color Post-It would trigger a rage full of curses and cryptic demands;

His venom-choked memos filled page after page in his favorite font: **Comic Sans**.

A misapplied paper-clip once
  set him tearing through cubicles
  wielding a broom;

He made Ricky cry seven times
  without caring in the space of
  just one afternoon.

When he screamed at Christine for
  a Scotch-tape mistake: "A moron
  could do your job better!"

It was finally more than the office
  could take—

They found (most of) Gene
  in the shredder.

The Martians beamed up Boris
for their interstellar zoo,

But estimated wrongly
his resistance:

He smashed the sonar, cracked the
warp core, broke the yoke in two

Killed the engine, crawled inside,
and hid the pistons.

All of this was charming
to the Martians hitherto;

They didn't rue their choice
of dirty human—

Till he mistook a matter-replicator
for the loo

And cleanup claimed the lives
of thirty crewmen.

Bernard was far more curious
   Than a little boy should be;
It made his mother furious
When he'd scamper off to see
What might be hiding in a tarp
Or maybe underneath a bin:
'Twas a nail so very sharp
It didn't hurt when it went in!
Just the latest of his treasures—
By now he'd built a fine collection.
So nice when hobbies give
   you pleasure
(Till you die of the infection).

"My finest batch yet,"
　　bragged Victor the brewer,

"As spicy as Bacchus'
　　own daughter—

High in foam, high in malt,
　　high in hops, but still fewer

Complex carbohydrates than water.

My crowning achievement!"
　　he bellowed out loud

In the self-assured way
　　he discussed things;

Still Simone was unsure: "Look,
　　it's great that you're proud,

But for pink lemonade,
　　it's disgusting!"

"Let's make it a deal,"
  the governor growled,
"The public will be none the wiser.
And should any do-gooder
  notice and howl,
I'll just blame my hapless adviser."

An agreement was met,
   and handshakes were shook-

"They won't dare to call *me* a liar!"

But justice was swift for
   His Honor the crook:

The teapot was wearing a wire.

The kettle gave evidence,
   all in good order,

That led to his speedy dismissal.

(But pity the miserable court
   reporter

Who had to transcribe all the
   whistles.)

Ever since the accident,
　　Rose had been perturbed

She'd sit out in the garden,
　　staring quietly at birds

She never said a word to them,
　　but fixed them with her eyes

And when they started staring
　　back, she didn't seem surprised.

They'd waddle closer every day,
　　then slowly peck her hands;

She'd whisper in their feathers
　　words we couldn't understand.

And when the winter came to drive
　　the flocks to southern climes,

A single tiny shoe was all
　　of her that we could find.

St. Whinge's Day was quite relaxing
On Y'haug'f'than
 I wept;
My verb for Verb Day
 was "begaxing"
And on Lethargy I slept.
My beard was quite
 appreciated
Though I regret not shaping it;
My waffles on St. Crêpe's
 I traded
For a bad relationship.

I made a sporknife
    on Just Make It

It helped me eat
    my pickles;

I laughed at those with
    faces naked

And swallowed a fistful
    of nickels.

I hope that you'll all
    do the same

As into a new year
    we delve!

(And if you forget these
    holidays' names

They're at:
    wondermark.com/holidays2012)

UNUSED VERSES
from prior years

The snow lay thick
  that winter morn

When Theo snuck outside—

His mom was sick,
  and he had sworn

To never leave her side.

But something in that chilly air

Had called his name for weeks.

Half a figure, not quite
  fully there,

Brought blood into his cheeks.

"Who's there?" he cried,
   in voice as hoarse

As dust, from years indoors;

(His ma'd been comatose,
   of course

Since Carter followed Ford.)

"It's me," he heard it said—
   By whom?

Impossible to tell:

"Your mother! I've been dead
   since June!"

(That would explain the smell.)

Fernand was a horse
 with congenital ills:
Small face, tiny teeth, lack of tail.
A veterinarian gave him
 some pills
But warned they were
 likely to fail.
"I've not seen a horse look
 as human as this;
No equine in your DNA!
My treament must call you
 a man, I insist—
A horse, after all, cannot pay."

Old Ricky had a factory
   that manufactured dreams

With rows of hopes and fears in
   bins that stacked up to the beams.

When someone fell asleep his
   mind would open and unfurl

From this gritty raw material Rick
   would craft, each night, a pearl.

But Ricky's now retiring, at age of
   sixty-five.

A robot will replace him—
   so the art will stay alive;

Ricky says he'll move to France.
   Maybe open up a winery?

But pretty soon the dreams of
   all the world will be in binary.

So what happens next?
  Where do we go from here?

I see you're perplexed;
  It's the end of the year.

I hope you're not blue—
  I'm not, and here's why!

We've made it both through!
  Yay, Team You & I!

We've weathered some trials.
  Yes, we've fought a few fights.

Put on some miles and
  scaled some new heights;

We battled a snake! Got the croup!
  Ate bug stew!

I can't wait for my next
  adventure with you.

www.ingramcontent.com/pod-product-compliance
Lightning Source LLC
Chambersburg PA
CBHW061327040426
42444CB00011B/2801